BROKEN FOR YOU

A CHRISTIAN HAGGADAH FOR PASSOVER

FOUNDED IN TRUTH
·YESHUA· FAMILY·
·FELLOWSHIP·

Broken For You: A Christian Haggadah For Passover

Copyright © 2019 Matthew Vander Els.
All rights reserved.

Publication rights Founded in Truth Fellowship

Publisher grants permission to reference short quotations (fewer than 300 words) in reviews, magazines, newspapers, websites, or other publications. Request for permission to reproduce more than 300 words can be made at: info@foundedintruth.com

Scripture quotations are from The ESV® Bible (The Holy Bible, English Standard Version®), copyright © 2001 by Crossway, a publishing ministry of Good News Publishers. Used by permission.

All rights reserved.

Founded in Truth
PO Box 38042, Rock Hill, SC 29732 USA
www.foundedintruth.com
Comments and questions: info@foundedintruth.com

WHAT IS PASSOVER?

This day shall be for you a memorial day, and you shall keep it as a feast to the Lord; throughout your generations, as a statute forever, you shall keep it as a feast.
-Exodus 12:14

Passover is a day that memorializes God's redemptive power and victory over forces of oppression. The story of Passover starts a long time ago in ancient Egypt. The Bible tells us in the book of Exodus that the Israelites found themselves enslaved under the oppressive regime of Pharoah and they cried out to God for redemption.

God responds by sending numerous plagues that crush the Egyptian empire. He then commands the Israelites to participate in a strange ceremony that involves taking a lamb, preparing it, and then killing it. The lamb must die, and the Israelites must eat its flesh and put its blood on the doorposts of their homes. The blood is a symbol of a covenant with God and protects them from a final plague sent upon Egypt, the messenger of death. The blood both saves them and grants them freedom.

The Israelites leave Egypt and travel three days into the wilderness. There God splits the Red Sea for them to cross through safely. The Apostle Paul calls this event the "baptism of Moses" (1 Cor. 10:2). The moment they walked through the waters, they were no longer slaves but became a nation birthed out of God's victorious redemption.

Jesus (Yeshua) speaks of this event during the Last Supper with His disciples (Mark 14:12-26) when He uses the symbols and the history of this story to explain how his death is going to change the world. He picks up the bread and says "eat of it; this is my flesh." He picks up the wine and says "drink of this; this is the blood of a new covenant." Something big is about to happen—something bigger than ever before. Redemption is coming in a way that will be similar to the first Passover, but its impact will be far greater.

This new, greater Exodus won't produce redemption from slavery to Egypt or freedom from the oppressive powers of Pharoah. This Exodus through Yeshua will produce redemption from slavery to sin and freedom from the oppressive forces of death, the things that hold our hearts captive and separate us from God.

Passover is a festival of freedom. For Christians, it is not simply a story about a people long ago who made their Exodus from Egypt. It is a story about a people making a greater Exodus from the oppressive powers of death and slavery to sin. It is the story of a lamb that entered the battle against the greatest evil and was victorious as if a lion had entered the battlefield (Rev 5:5-6).

Broken For You: A Christian Haggadah For Passover

Where do we start?

As we prepare for this memorial of the true Passover Lamb, Yeshua, we also prepare our hearts and our homes.

That's right, our homes too! Passover kicks off a week-long festival known as the Feast of Unleavened Bread. It's a week where you are to refrain from eating any leavened bread.

Seven days you shall eat unleavened bread. On the first day, you shall remove leaven out of your houses … and you shall observe the Feast of Unleavened Bread, for on this very day I brought your hosts out of the land of Egypt.
-Exodus 2:15, 17

Why do we need to remove leavening from our homes? Leavening represents the things that give rise to a life without God. Sin, pride, and those things within the human heart that distance us from God. God is giving us a clear picture of how transforming and life-changing His redemption is. The way we lived before has died, for we are a new creation.

Broken For You: A Christian Haggadah For Passover

The Apostle Paul said:

> *Your boasting is not good. Don't you know that a little leavening leavens the whole batch of dough? Get rid of the old leavening, so that you may be a new unleavened batch—as you really are. For Christ, our Passover lamb, has been sacrificed. Therefore let us keep the Festival, not with the old bread leavened with malice and wickedness, but with the unleavened bread of sincerity and truth.*
> *-1 Cor. 5:6-8*

This practice is a ritual that depicts the purging of the leavening from our homes, but should also reflect, more importantly, the purging of our hearts and the auditing of who we are and what our character is in light of what Jesus has done for us.

As we prepare our homes and our hearts for Passover, the week of unleavened bread, and the day of First Fruits, we need to remember that this is not about a lamb that was sacrificed in Egypt. This is not about bunnies and eggs and baskets of candy, either. As believers, this practice revolves around who this person of Yeshua is in our lives and it should orbit His redemptive love. This should be a time of celebration, fun, and excitement. Why? Because Passover is the festival of Freedom. Not from slavery in Egypt, or the oppressive powers of Pharoah, but freedom from slavery to sin and the oppressive power of death in this present evil age. We celebrate the victory through God's supreme love, grace, mercy, and forgiveness.

ORDER OF THE EVENING

Removal of Leavening
Prepare the table
The Seder Elements
The Seder

Removal of Leavening

How do we get "leavening" out of our homes? Great question, because it is not as easy as you think. Most people think of leavening as being in bread only. And while bread is typically where you find leavening, you find it in a lot of unlikely places too.

The Hebrew word that is translated as "leavening" in the Bible is seor, which actually means starter dough. That is flour and water made into dough and left out for the natural yeast in the air to ferment. This dough is then added to a larger batch of dough to leaven it. So, bread, pancakes, cake, cookies, some pasta, all must be removed from the home for the week.

The kitchen is not the only place that you will find chametz or leavened food hiding. We also find it in our air vents, our couch cushions, and in the corners of your room. It is EVERYWHERE! So are our desires to pursue things outside of God's reign, such as sin. For Christians, cleaning out your home of leavened products is a truly deep time of reflection as well as a teaching moment for your children.

The point is not to simply get everything out of your home.

If you get every crumb of leavening out of your home and still have arrogance, malice, and unforgiveness in your heart, then you have achieved nothing. This practice needs to reflect what is happening in your heart, not simply your home.

Prepare the Table

Because Passover is a special time, special preparation is encouraged for the table and atmosphere. Lay out the table cloth. Place the nicer dishes out. Light some candles. Show the family that tonight will be different.

The Seder Elements

Traditionally, a special plate known as a "Seder plate" is placed on the table. This plate holds five symbolic items that help us remember why Passover is so important. If you do not own a Seder plate, you can simply use a regular plate.

1. **The roasted lamb shank bone** (Zeroa in Hebrew).
   The shank bone represents the Passover lamb peace offering.
2. **A roasted egg** (Beitzah in Hebrew)
   The roasted egg represents the haggigah or festival offerings roasted along with the Passover offering. After the destruction of the Temple, symbols for the Passover offering and Haggigah offerings were used on the Seder plate. An egg was chosen to make a stark distinction from the Passover symbol of the shank bone.
3. **The green vegetable** (Karpos in Hebrew)
   The karpos is typically celery or parsley. It represents the betrayal of Joseph by his brothers.
4. **Charoset**
   A mixture of nuts, apples, wine, and spices that represent the mortar used by the Israelites to build the cities of Egypt.
5. **Bitter Herbs** (Maror in Hebrew)
   Bitter herbs, which are usually horseradish or romaine lettuce, represents the bitterness of slavery.

Place small portions of each item on the seder plate for display purposes. Make sure you have enough for each participant in a separate container.

Matzah

Matzah is a piece of crispy unleavened bread. Each participant will need about two pieces of matzah during the seder. Traditionally, three extra pieces of matzah are then taken and placed in a special bag for later use in the seder.

The Four Cups of Wine

Wine has been a traditional aspect of the Passover Seder for thousands of years. Matthew, Mark, and Luke seem to indicate the Last Supper was a Passover meal that Jesus had with His disciples where wine took on the symbolism of Yeshua's own covenant blood.

At a traditional Passover Seder, each participant drinks four cups of wine or grape juice. The four cups remind us of the four expressions of redemption mentioned in Exodus 6:6-7.

1. I will bring you out from under the oppression of the Egyptians.
2. I will deliver you from slavery to them.
3. I will redeem you with an outstretched arm and with mighty acts of judgement.
4. I will take you to be my people.

Hand Washing

It is customary to begin the Seder with hand washing. This reminds us of the purity in God's Temple and how the priests washed before approaching God. Prepare by having a large bowl of water available for participants to dip their hands in.

Salt Water

Have a small bowl of salt water available at the beginning of the Seder to dip the karpos in.

Begin the Seder

The elements of the Seder are meant to be reminders, not the main course. Prepare a nice meal for everyone to celebrate together. Beef brisket or chicken are popular meals served during the Seder. You will not see lamb typically served for the Passover Seder meal. The Passover Lamb was a sacrifice that was allowed to be slaughtered and eaten only in Jerusalem. Most do not serve lamb as the main course due to not wanting to appear like they are eating the actual holy Passover sacrifice.

Summary of the Seder

1. Kaddesh - Opening prayer
2. Urchatz - Hand washing
3. Karpas - Dip the parsley in salt water
4. Yachatz - Break the matzah
5. Maggid - Tell the Exodus story and the story of Yeshua
6. Motzi - Blessing over the bread
7. Matzah - Eating Matzah
8. Maror - Bitter herbs
9. Korech - Matzah and bitter herbs together
10. Shulchan Orech - Serve the main meal
11. Eat the hidden matzah!
12. Barech - Give thanks to God!
13. Hallel - Sing songs together
14. Nirtzah - Conclusion

Let's begin.

Broken For You: A Christian Haggadah For Passover

Now on the first day of Unleavened Bread the disciples came to Jesus, saying, "Where will you have us prepare for you to eat the Passover?" He said, "Go into the city to a certain man and say to him, 'The Teacher says, My time is at hand. I will keep the Passover at your house with my disciples.'" And the disciples did as Jesus had directed them, and they prepared the Passover.
-Matt. 26:17-19

Kadesh - Opening Prayer

Leader: And He took the cup, and gave thanks, and said, Take this, and divide it among yourselves: For I say unto you, I will not drink of the fruit of the vine, until the kingdom of God shall come. (Luke 22:17-18)

Leader: We give thanks this day to you, God of creation. For you have redeemed us from the oppressive powers of death and freed us from slavery to sin. You have provided the greatest Exodus through the blood of the Passover, Yeshua.

The First Cup

Pour first cup of wine or grape juice

Leader: Blessed are you, O Lord, our God, King of the universe, who has created the fruit of the vine.

Hebrew: *Baruch atah, Adonai Eloheinu, Melech haolam, borei p'ri hagafen.*

All: Amen in the name of Yeshua!

Leader: Blessed are you, King of creation, who has sanctified us through your living word. Who has appointed times of remembrance and celebration. Be with us as we join you in celebrating your redemptive love through the Passover Seder as we recall the time in ancient Egypt where the Israelites were slaves, but also as we recall our own exodus from slavery to sin.

All: Amen, in the name of Yeshua!

Drink the first cup of wine.

During the time of Jesus, participants leaned due to the Romanized table setting. This tradition of leaning with eating symbolizes being at ease and joyful. The tradition continues even today.

URCHATZ - The Hand Washing

Pass a large bowl of water around the table, allowing each participant to dip their hands in the water and dry them with a towel.

Leader: "Who may ascend the mountain of the Lord? Who may stand in His holy place? The one who has clean hands and a pure heart, who does not trust in an idol or swear by a false god." (Psa. 24:3-4)

Karpas

All participants take a small piece of celery or parsley and dip it into the salt water bowl, but don't eat it yet.

Leader: Blessed are you, Lord our God, King of the universe, who creates the fruit of the earth.

Hebrew: *Baruch atah Adonai Eloheinu melech ha-olam borei p'ri ha-adama.*

All: Amen in the name of Yeshua!

Eat the parsley.

YACHATZ - Breaking the matzah

The leader takes the three special pieces of matzah set aside at the beginning of the seder. Remove the middle piece of matzah and hold it up. Break the piece in half. Take the large of the two broken pieces, wrap it in a napkin and set it aside. This piece will now be known as the Afikomen, a Greek word meaning something special and joyous.

Just like Yeshua was broken, wrapped, and buried, we take this special piece of matzah that was broken, wrap it up, and hide it away.

MAGGID - Tell the story!
(Story intentionally simplified for children)

Every participant lifts a piece of Matzah.

Leader: This is the bread of affliction (Deut. 16:3) that the Israelites ate when they left Egypt. This is a bread that is absent of leavening representing the absence of Egypt in our lives. Let all who are hungry come and eat! Let all who are needy come and celebrate God's redemption! We are no longer slaves but free.

Set the matzah down.

All participants pour the second cup of wine or grape juice.

The Four Questions

The youngest child that is able to read should ask these questions:

1. This night is so different than other nights. On other nights, we can eat regular bread. Tonight, why do we eat only matzah?

2. On other nights, we eat other vegetables. Tonight, why do we eat bitter herbs?

3. On other nights, we do not have to dip our food at all. Tonight, why do we dip our food twice?

4. On other nights, we do not sit in a certain way. Tonight, why do we recline or lean?

Leader: Well, I am glad you asked.

Tonight is special because we remember the power of God's redemption. We will now retell the story of the Exodus (Exodus 12:24-28).

The Israelites were slaves to Pharaoh in Egypt. Task masters were set over them and they were forced to do heavy work and were oppressed daily. They cried out to God and He answered!

God sent ten mighty plagues against Egypt, defeating the evil pharaoh and the oppressive powers of Egypt. These are the ten plagues God sent:

Remove one drop of wine from your cup using your finger and let it drop on a piece of matzah every time a plague is mentioned.

Dam - Blood
Tzefardea - Frogs
Kinnim - Lice
Arov - Wild Animals
Dever - Disease on livestock
Shechin - Boils
Barad - Hail
Arbeh - Locusts
Choshech - Darkness
Makkot Bechorot - Death of the Firstborn

Before the final plague, God told the Israelites to do something very important. They were to sacrifice a lamb, place its blood on the doorposts of their home, and eat the flesh of the lamb. The Bible tells us (Exodus 12:23) that the LORD passed over the homes when He saw the blood, protecting them from the angel of death that came upon the firstborns of Egypt.

It was through the blood of the lamb that the Israelites were redeemed from a life of slavery and the plague of death.

Leader: After the ten plagues, The Israelites fled Egypt. They came to a huge sea, but the Lord split the Red Sea in half, which allowed the Israelites to cross on dry land, entering a new life of liberty.

They were given the Torah at Mt. Sinai, representing a new way of living as God's people.

This was the first Exodus, but not the last. Jeremiah 23:5-8 tells us of a coming King that God will establish, a "new Moses" that will conquer the oppressive powers governing God's people. This will be a greater Exodus that will result in all of God's people being reconciled back to him, ending the exile from God's presence.

As believers, we know this King to be Yeshua, the true Son of God. Yeshua taught us what it means to truly follow God with our hearts. He proclaimed the birth of God's Kingdom on earth, performed miracles, and birthed the promises of God that were prophesied by Isaiah, Jeremiah, and Malachi. When Passover came and the lamb was to be slain to remind us of God's redemption, it was Yeshua that died, birthing a new type of Passover, a greater Passover just as Jeremiah 23:7

says.

The story of Yeshua does not end there. After Yeshua was crucified for the sins of the world, He was taken off the cross and buried. The world thought it had lost the appointed Son of God. But three days later something amazing happened. The grave that held His body broke open and Yeshua walked out. By God's power, Yeshua had conquered death and He invited everyone to follow Him and share in that same life giving power. This is what Passover means to Christians. It means celebrating the power of our God and the life-giving presence of Yeshua!

> *Get rid of the old yeast, so that you may be a new unleavened batch—as you really are. For Christ, our Passover lamb, has been sacrificed.*
> *-1 Cor. 5:7*

Passover is a festival of freedom—freedom from sin, death, and the oppressive powers of this present evil age.

MATZAH - Unleavened Bread

When God redeemed Israel from Egypt, they left in haste. This did not give them enough time to let any dough rise to make leavened bread (Exodus 12:33-34). Because of this, God commanded His people to remove all leavened bread from their lives during Passover and the week of Unleavened Bread. Instead, we are to eat unleavened bread (Lev 23:6).

So, too, we remember Yeshua who was not leavened with sin but bore our sins in order to redeem us (1 Peter 2:24).

Everyone holds up a piece of Matzah.

Leader: Blessed are you, Lord our God, King of the universe, who brings forth bread from the earth.

Hebrew: *Baruch atah Adonai Eloheinu melech ha-olam hamotzi lechem min.*

Put matzah down.

Maror - The Bitter Herbs

Raise bitter herbs.

The bitter herbs remind us of the bitterness of slavery as well as the oppressive powers of sin in our own lives. God commanded His people to eat the bitter herbs every year at Passover along with the matzah and Passover lamb (Numbers 9:11).

Put bitter herbs down.

> *You shall tell your son on that day, 'It is because of what the Lord did for me when I came out of Egypt.*
> *-Exodus 13:8*

In every generation, a person should try to imagine that it was they themselves that were brought out of Egypt. This is something that many struggle with, as the event told in the Book of Exodus was so long ago. As believers, we have experienced an Exodus event within our lifetime. We have experienced the power of the blood of the lamb, the power of God's strength, the defeat of principalities, and we have experienced God's complete redemptive work through Yeshua. We are no longer slaves to sin. (Romans 6:17-18)

Broken For You: A Christian Haggadah For Passover

Give Praise

Lift second cup of wine.

For this reason, we give honor, praise, gratitude, and blessing to elevate the name of our King above all names and to give complete glory to the one who not only performed the miracles for our forefathers in Egypt but also saved us. Let it be known that our God keeps His promises and is the savior of all!

The Second Cup

Leader: Blessed are you, O Lord, our God, King of the universe, who has created the fruit of the vine.

Hebrew: *Baruch atah, Adonai Eloheinu, Melech haolam, borei p'ri hagafen.*

All: Amen, in the name of Yeshua!

Drink the second cup.

Eat the Matzah.

Leader: We eat this bread to remind us of the greatest Exodus performed by the power of God.

Take a bite of the matzah you were just holding up.

Eat the Bitter Herbs

Leader: Blessed are you, Lord our God, who has commanded us to eat the bitter herbs.

All: Amen, in the name of Yeshua!

Place a generous amount of horse radish or lettuce on the matzah and eat.

Note: It is an honorable pursuit to bring a tear to your eye as a result of the bitter herbs. Generous helpings help.

Matzah Sandwich

Place the bitter herbs on one piece of matzah and place some charoset on another. Combine them together to make a sandwich and enjoy!

You may eat the bitter herbs and charoset freely from this time forward in the Seder.

SHULCAN ORECH - The Main Course is Served

Serve and eat the main course. Enjoy the fellowship with your family and friends.

Traditional Passover Seder meals include matzah ball soup, beef brisket, and chicken. Remember, no food should contain leavening in this entire meal.

Leader: Father, we thank you for this time together as your family. We thank you for the opportunity to reflect on your redemptive love, and we thank you for the food we have here before us. Allow your spirit of peace, love, and joy to overtake our hearts as we remember the true Passover, Yeshua (Jesus) the Messiah.

All: Amen in the name of Yeshua!

Break for the meal and return when everyone is finished eating

Broken For You: A Christian Haggadah For Passover

The Third Cup and TZAFUN
(The Hidden Matzah)

Leader: "For I received from the Lord what I also passed on to you: The Lord Jesus, on the night He was betrayed, took bread, and when He had given thanks, He broke it and said, "This is my body, which is for you; do this in remembrance of me." In the same way, after supper He took the cup, saying, "This cup is the new covenant in my blood; do this, whenever you drink it, in remembrance of me." For whenever you eat this bread and drink this cup, you proclaim the Lord's death until he comes." (1 Cor. 11:23-26)

Take the piece of matzah you wrapped in the napkin at the beginning of the Seder and unwrap it. Break off a piece for every believer at the table.

Everyone pours the third cup of wine or grape juice and holds the piece of matzah

Leader: Paul instructs us to partake in a rite set forth by Yeshua Himself. At the Last Supper, Yeshua held up the bread and broke it. He held up the cup of wine and said to drink it. "This is my body. This is my blood." It was here at the Passover that Yeshua reveals Himself as the ultimate Passover sacrifice. The lamb that was not only slain but consumed in order to give life (Exodus 12:8). The blood remains a sign of overpowering death and entering into new life.

Leader: Yeshua said, "This is my body, broken for you. Do this in remembrance of me." (1 Cor. 11:24, Mark 14:22)

Everyone Eat a piece of matzah and hold up third cup of wine or grape juice.

Leader: Yeshua said, "This is my blood of the new covenant, poured out for many. Do this in remembrance of me." (1 Cor. 11:25, Mark 14:24)

Everyone drink from the third cup of wine or grape juice

Leader: Let us remember at this moment that the power of God knows no limits. The salvation of God is manifest through Yeshua. Tonight, we celebrate the Passover remembering the ultimate Lamb, the lamb that takes away the sins of the world, granting freedom for all. Yeshua, our King.

HALLEL - Psalms of Praise

Feel free to include your own favorite songs of praise.

Psalm 118

1 Oh give thanks to the Lord, for he is good;
for his steadfast love endures forever!

2 Let Israel say, "His steadfast love endures forever."

3 Let the house of Aaron say, "His steadfast love endures forever."

4 Let those who fear the Lord say, "His steadfast love endures forever."

5 Out of my distress I called on the Lord; the Lord answered me and set me free. 6 The Lord is on my side; I will not fear. What can man do to me?

7 The Lord is on my side as my helper; I shall look in triumph on those who hate me. 8 It is better to take refuge in the Lord than to trust in man.

9 It is better to take refuge in the Lord than to trust in princes.

10 All nations surrounded me; in the name of the Lord I cut them off!

11 They surrounded me, surrounded me on every side; in the name of the Lord I cut them off! 12 They surrounded me like bees; they went out like a fire among thorns; in the name of the Lord I cut them off!

13 I was pushed hard, so that I was falling, but the Lord helped me.

14 The Lord is my strength and my song; he has become my salvation.

15 Glad songs of salvation are in the tents of the righteous: "The right hand of the Lord does valiantly, 16 the right hand of the Lord exalts, the right hand of the Lord does valiantly!"

17 I shall not die, but I shall live, and recount the deeds of the Lord.
18 The Lord has disciplined me severely, but he has not given me over to death. 19 Open to me the gates of righteousness, that I may enter through them and give thanks to the Lord. 20 This is the gate of the Lord;
the righteous shall enter through it. 21 I thank you that you have answered me and have become my salvation. 22 The stone that the builders rejected has become the cornerstone. 23 This is the Lord's doing; it is marvelous in our eyes. 24 This is the day that the Lord has made;
let us rejoice and be glad in it. 25 Save us, we pray, O Lord!
O Lord, we pray, give us success! 26 Blessed is he who comes in the name of the Lord! We bless you from the house of the Lord.
27 The Lord is God, and he has made his light to shine upon us.
Bind the festal sacrifice with cords, up to the horns of the altar!
28 You are my God, and I will give thanks to you; you are my God; I will extol you. 29 Oh give thanks to the Lord, for he is good; for his steadfast love endures forever!

Psalm 98

1 Oh sing to the Lord a new song,
for he has done marvelous things!
His right hand and his holy arm
have worked salvation for him.
2 The Lord has made known his salvation;
he has revealed his righteousness in the sight of the nations.
3 He has remembered his steadfast love and faithfulness

to the house of Israel.
All the ends of the earth have seen
the salvation of our God.
4 Make a joyful noise to the Lord, all the earth;
break forth into joyous song and sing praises!
5 Sing praises to the Lord with the lyre,
with the lyre and the sound of melody!
6 With trumpets and the sound of the horn
make a joyful noise before the King, the Lord!
7 Let the sea roar, and all that fills it;
the world and those who dwell in it!
8 Let the rivers clap their hands;
let the hills sing for joy together
9 before the Lord, for he comes
to judge the earth.
He will judge the world with righteousness,
and the peoples with equity.

The Fourth Cup

Everyone pours fourth cup of wine or grape juice

Leader: Blessed are you, O Lord, our God, King of the universe, who has created the fruit of the vine.

Hebrew: *Baruch atah, Adonai Eloheinu, Melech haolam, borei p'ri hagafen.*

All: Amen in the name of Yeshua!

Drink fourth cup of wine or grape juice

Leader: Tonight as we have remembered the salvation of our God. We have broken the bread and drank the wine. With four cups of wine we remember the fulfillment of God's promises:

1. He has brought us out from under the oppression of death.
2. He has delivered us from slavery to sin.
3. He has redeemed us with an outstretched arm and with mighty acts of judgement.
4. He has taken us to be His.

For you are bought with a price: therefore glorify God in your body, and in your spirit, which are God's."
-1 Cor 6:20

ALL: Leshanah Haba'ah Birusha'Lay'Yim

Next year in Jerusalem!

לשנה הבאה בירושלים

Broken For You: A Christian Haggadah For Passover

ABOUT FOUNDED IN TRUTH

Founded in Truth is a Yeshua centered fellowship located in Fort Mill, SC. We are passionate about the power of the gospel, the testimony of Yeshua, and the sacredness of the Bible. At Founded in Truth, we thrive as a community built on the three pillars below.

Yeshua/Jesus

We are a community formed by the teachings, life, death, and resurrection of a rabbi from Nazareth named Yeshua (Jesus). It is through His spirit by which we find our common bond. Through the paradox of His death on the cross, we see the way to God's love, the truth of all He is, and the life that only He can provide – one that is eternal. The gospel of Yeshua is the foundation for our community locally and beyond.

Family

If there is one thing we celebrate at Founded in Truth, it is family. Whether your household is small or large, local or far away, you are invited to take your place here with us. We thrive together to build up an atmosphere that shows forth God's love in an authentic way not just to be a fellowship but also to teach the children in the community what being an image bearer is all about.

Fellowship

We value each other. In the Beginning, God said it was not good for man to be alone. We were meant for fellowship, and we believe when we come together, we celebrate God's goodness, promises, and grace. We know God has called our lives to intersect, so what better way to fulfill the command of scripture to love one another?

Our vision is to exist to build a community that bears the image of God and lives the redeemed life Yeshua gives.

We pray we can do this by empowering the world with the knowledge of the Gospel, offering the discipleship in Torah, and demonstrating how to humbling Walk of Yeshua to the world around us.

If this haggadah has been edifying to you or you would like to partner with us to carry out the vision above, we ask first and foremost for prayer. The guidance and wisdom from God are what we desire the most.

We would also ask that you consider donating to Founded in Truth. You can give online through our website at www.FoundedinTruth.com or send a personal check made out to

Founded in Truth to:
Founded in Truth
P.O. Box 38042
Rock Hill, SC 39732

Broken For You: A Christian Haggadah For Passover

Broken For You: A Christian Haggadah For Passover

Made in the USA
Las Vegas, NV
18 March 2025